The Story of Flight
SEAPLANES
And Naval Aviation

Crabtree Publishing Company
www.crabtreebooks.com

PMB 16A, 350 Fifth Avenue,
Suite 3308
New York, NY 10118

612 Welland Avenue
St. Catharines, Ontario
L2M 5V6

Published in 2004 by
Crabtree Publishing Company

Coordinating editor: Ellen Rodger
Project editors: Sean Charlebois, Carrie Gleason
Production coordinator: Rose Gowsell

Created and Produced by
David West Children's Books

Project Development, Design, and Concept
David West Children's Books:
Designer: Rob Shone
Editor: Gail Bushnell
Illustrators: Martyn Patrick, Terry Pastor, Gary Slater & Steve Weston (Specs Art), James Field & Mike Lacey (SGA), Alain Salesse (Contact Jupiter)
Picture Research: Carlotta Cooper

Photo Credits:
Abbreviations: t-top, m-middle, b-bottom, r-right, l-left, c-center.

Front cover & pages 4, 6, 8t, 20 - Royal Air Force Museum. 5 (Ian Loasby), 7, 8b, 10t, 16, 18, 22 (Anthony R. Dalton), 25, 28b - The Flight Collection. 12 - Boeing. 14 - Rex Features. 15, 21 - The Culture Archive. 24, 27t & b - Corbis Images. 28t - BOTEC® Ingenieursozietät GmbH.

06 05 04 03
10 9 8 7 6 5 4 3 2 1

Printed and bound in Dubai

Library of Congress Cataloging-in-Publication Data
Hansen, Ole Steen.
Seaplanes and naval aviation / written by Ole Steen Hansen.
p. cm. -- (The story of flight)
Summary: Describes aircraft that take off from ships or land on water and their use in military action and rescue, as well as for scientific research and commercial purposes.
Includes bibliographical references and index.
ISBN 0-7787-1209-5 (RLB : alk. paper) -- ISBN 0-7787-1225-7 (PB : alk. paper)
1. Seaplanes--Juvenile literature. 2. Naval aviation--Juvenile literature. [1. Seaplanes. 2. Aeronautics, Military.] I. Title. II. Series.
VG90.H36 2003
629.133'347--dc22

2003016177

The Story of Flight

SEAPLANES

And Naval Aviation

Ole Steen Hansen

Crabtree Publishing Company
www.crabtreebooks.com

CONTENTS

CONSOLIDATED CATALINA
The Catalina is one of the greatest flying boats in history. More Catalinas were built than all the other flying boats combined!

INTRODUCTION

From the very beginning of aviation, pilots have flown over or taken off from water. The first ever flight from water took place in 1910 when Henri Fabre flew his Hydravion near Marseilles, France. During wars, aircraft were used to protect friendly ships and attack enemy ships. Today, crossing an ocean by plane is far faster than by boat.

ON FLOATS
Many smaller aircraft, such as the Cessna 206 (above), are equipped with floats for landing on water.

WORLD'S FIRST SEAPLANE
When he was 28 years old, Henri Fabre made his first flight in his Hydravion.

PIONEERS

The world's first regular and scheduled air route was flown by a flying boat. The St. Petersburg-Tampa Airboat Line crossed the 22 miles (35 km) over Tampa Bay in Western Florida much faster than ships.

CURTIS SEAPLANES
In 1911, American Glenn Hammond Curtis flew his Hydroplane, a float plane and the world's first seaplane. One of his later flying boats is shown here.

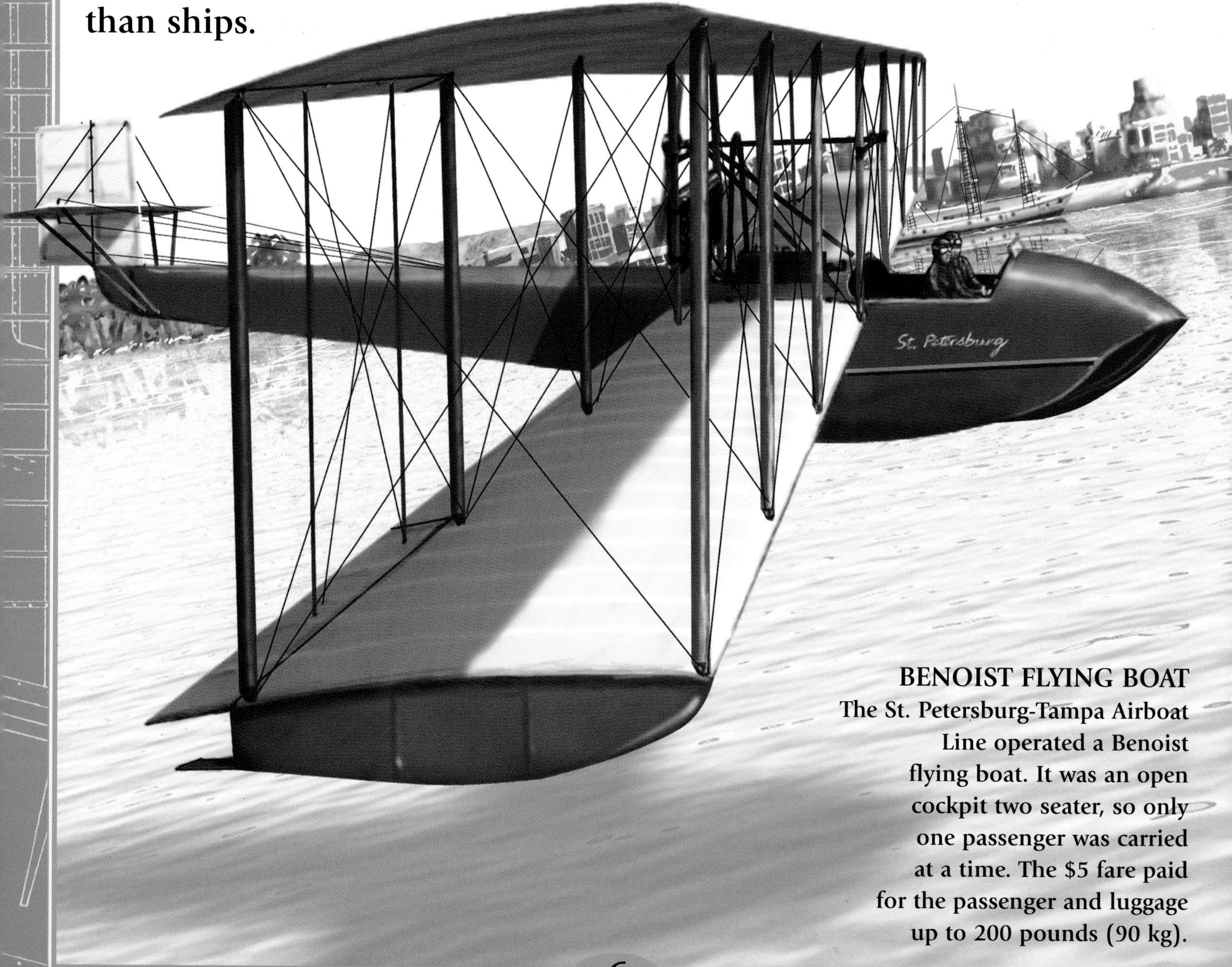

St. Petersburg

BENOIST FLYING BOAT
The St. Petersburg-Tampa Airboat Line operated a Benoist flying boat. It was an open cockpit two seater, so only one passenger was carried at a time. The $5 fare paid for the passenger and luggage up to 200 pounds (90 kg).

Seaplane Air Race
Before **World War I**, seaplane air races were held. A REP Monoplane is seen here at the St. Malo-Jersey race, in the English Channel, in 1912. A Monaco seaplane competition turned into an international contest for the Schneider Trophy. In the 1920s this contest helped make seaplanes the fastest aircraft in the world.

Pilot Tony Janus opened the new air route on January 1, 1914. The first passenger was A. C. Pfeil, the mayor of St. Petersburg. The normal fare was $5, but Pfeil bid $400 to be the first airline passenger ever. The flying boat cruised at around 62 miles per hour (100 km/h), making it a windy experience for Janus and Pfeil. The distance across the bay was 22 miles (35 km) and was covered in 23 minutes. The Airboat Line operated two regular daily return flights. Only eighteen departures had to be cancelled due to weather and just four due to mechanical troubles. Unfortunately, it was difficult for the airline to afford to keep operating, so after four months it had to close.

Douglas DWC (Float Plane)

Douglas DF-151 (Flying Boat)

Consolidated PBY-5A (Amphibian)

FLOAT PLANES, FLYING BOATS, AND AMPHIBIANS

Float planes use floats to land on water. A flying boat has a **hull** that floats like a boat on water. The hull must be strong, since landing on water puts great strain on the airframe. Amphibians are flying boats with retractable wheels that also allow them to land on a runway.

AT WAR OVER THE SEA

During World War I, an aircraft's most important work during a land battle was to observe enemy positions. Over the sea, aircraft also observed enemy ships, and directed warships toward them.

SHIP-BOARD PLANES
HMS Empress was a cross-Channel ship hastily modified to carry seaplanes at the outbreak of World War I.

Over the seas, planes played a role in battles by entering into combat against enemy planes, and dropping small bombs and torpedoes at targets. Early in the war, seaplanes were carried on ships into the water. After taking off, these planes followed the battle fleets and watched out for the ships down below. Later, the British navy started to build aircraft carriers, which were ships that allowed faster aircraft with wheels to take off from their decks.

REPAIRS AT SEA
The June 1918 air battle started when one Felixstowe landed on the water with engine trouble. The German patrol attacked it, and the other British flying boats fought back. Afterward, the crew repaired the Felixstowe and returned to base.

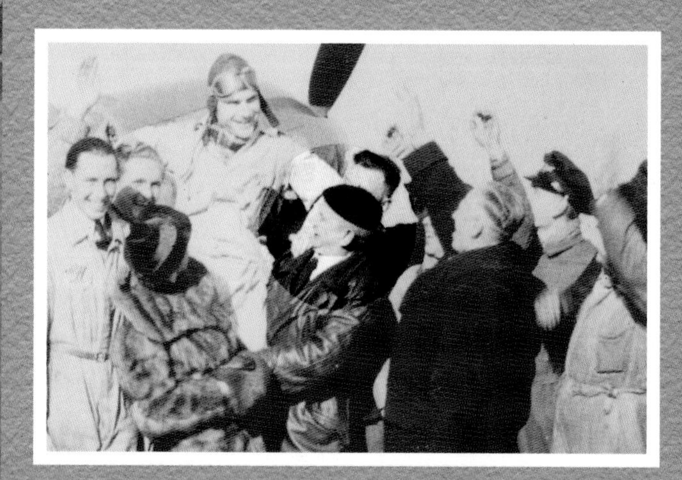

A seaplane air battle was fought over the North Sea on June 4, 1918. Five Felixstowe F.2A flying boats fought fifteen German float planes. The British pilots pulled their 5.5 ton (4,989 kg) flying boats around easily, shooting down two German seaplanes and damaging four more. All the Felixstowes returned to their base in Britain.

SHORT TYPE 184

In 1915, British Short Type 184 float planes used torpedoes to sink Turkish ships. This was the first time aircraft had succeeded in doing so. One of the ships sunk after the aircraft had landed on the water with engine problems. The aircraft **taxied** toward the Turkish ship, released the torpedo, and sank it.

Ernst Heinkel

German designer Ernst Heinkel designed float planes during World War I. The Hansa-Brandenburg W.12 biplane and the W.29 monoplane (seen here in the main illustration) were both his designs. After the war, Ernst Heinkel started his own company and designed a series of sleek and fast aircraft. In 1939, his Heinkel He 100 flew at 464 miles per hour (746 km/h), establishing a new world speed record (shown at left).

FLYING IN STYLE

Before World War II, many air routes were flown by flying boats. It was considered a safety feature that the aircraft could land on water if they had mechanical problems. They could also land near harbors and cities that did not yet have airports.

BOEING 314
The Boeing 314 Clipper went into service just before World War II. These large flying boats had compartments that could be turned into sleeping units with berths at night. They also had a dining room, galley, dressing rooms, and toilets. They were used on both Atlantic and Pacific routes.

Service on board these early flying boats was much different than on today's airliners. Cooks worked in **galleys** making the food on board, whereas on today's airlines the food is just heated up on the plane.

Savoia-Marchetti Formation
Italian military flying boats created a sensation on some long distance flights. In 1930, twelve Savoia-Marchetti S.55s flew from Rome to Rio de Janeiro – a distance of 6,500 miles (10,460 km). Three years later, 25 S.55s flew from Rome to the World's Fair in Chicago. These flights were not non-stop, but they were impressive, because flying across the Atlantic was still risky and these Italian aviators did it in large formations!

When Empire flying boats refueled off Crete, a Greek island in the Mediterranean Sea, the passengers had tea in a luxurious yacht while waiting. On U.S. flying boats, passengers could also enjoy a self-service area with ice water and throw-away paper cups. The down side was that these early passenger planes were much noisier than the cabins of today's jets. Cotton wool to put in the ears and sick bags were often needed, since the planes flew in **turbulence** at lower **altitudes**.

ALL THE COMFORTS OF HOME

The Short "C" Class flying boats were extremely luxurious, but for the rich only. They carried just seventeen passengers because they also had to carry two tons (1,614 kg) of mail.

1 Cockpit
2 Lounge
3 Main hold
4 Galley
5 Midship cabin
6 Promenade deck
7 Rear cabin
8 Rear hold

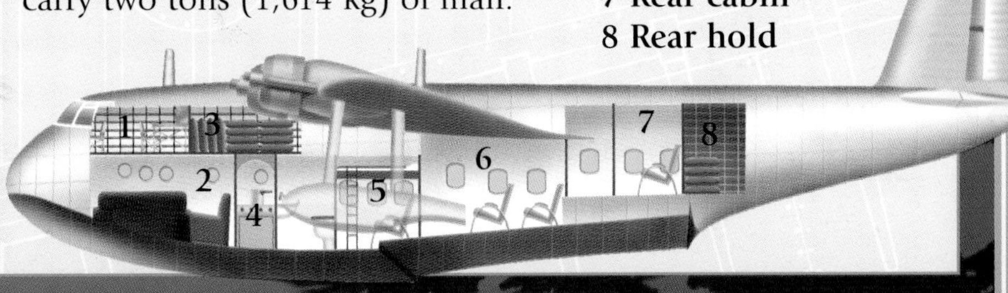

EXOTIC PLACES

Compared to today's jet liners, flying boats such as the Short Calcutta (shown at top), flew low and slow and offered passengers a view of exotic places around the world.

SMALL SEAPLANES

While large flying boats were spanning the globe, smaller seaplanes were also being developed. Some small seaplanes held world speed records, others did useful work. Aircraft such as the "Duck" were designed as seaplanes, while others were land planes with floats.

HUBBARD AND BOEING
In 1919, pilot Eddie Hubbard convinced aircraft builder William E. Boeing that money could be made flying mail between Seattle, Washington, and Vancouver, British Columbia. Boeing is still producing aircraft, such as the large Boeing 747 jet airliner.

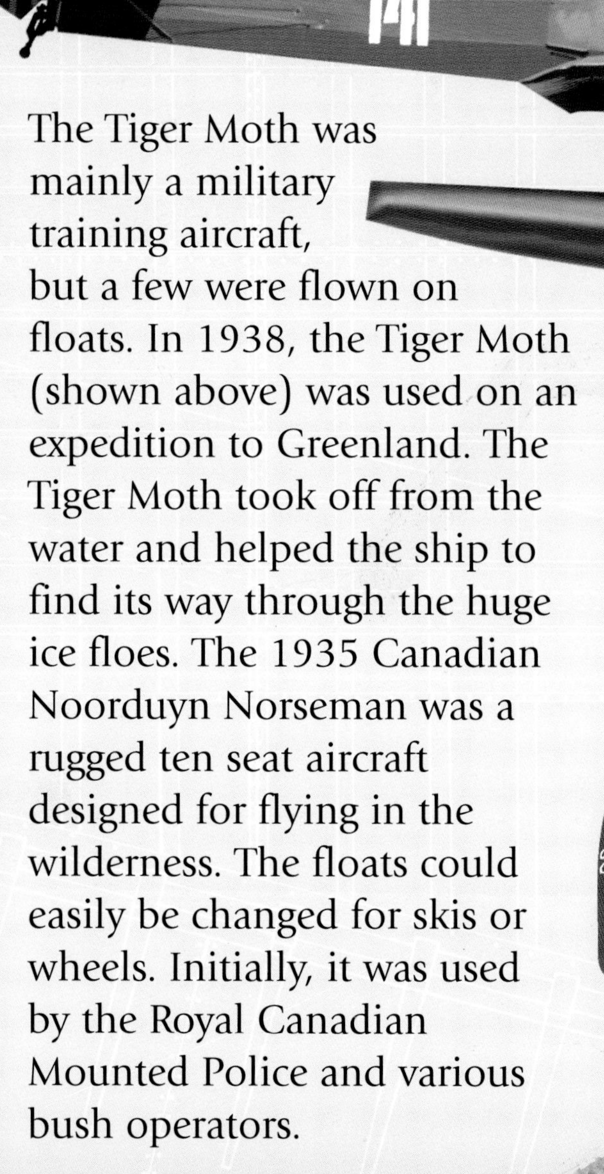

The Tiger Moth was mainly a military training aircraft, but a few were flown on floats. In 1938, the Tiger Moth (shown above) was used on an expedition to Greenland. The Tiger Moth took off from the water and helped the ship to find its way through the huge ice floes. The 1935 Canadian Noorduyn Norseman was a rugged ten seat aircraft designed for flying in the wilderness. The floats could easily be changed for skis or wheels. Initially, it was used by the Royal Canadian Mounted Police and various bush operators.

TIGER MOTH FLOAT PLANE
Length: 26 ft (7.9 m)
Wingspan: 29 ft 4 in (8.9 m)
Speed: 109 mph (175 km/h)

FLYING RADIATOR
The Supermarine S6B flew at 408 mph (656 km/h), making it the world's fastest aircraft in 1931. Cooling the engine was a problem. Cooling water circulated between the double layers of the wing covering. It was also circulated on the float surfaces. The engine oil was cooled in tubes running down the **fuselage** and in the tail fin.

Water radiators

Oil radiators

NOORDUYN NORSEMAN
Length: 33 ft 1 in (10.1 m)
Wingspan: 51 ft 8 in (15.7 m)
Speed: 148 mph (238 km/h)

Francesco De Pinedo
Italian aviator Francesco De Pinedo believed seaplanes were the aircraft of the future. He said: "The world's principal cities are mirrored by seas, rivers or lakes. Why not utilize these immense, ready-to-use, natural air strips in place of costly airports?" In 1925, he flew a Savoia S-16ter (shown at left) from Italy to Tokyo and Australia. In 1927 he also flew a S.55 flying boat named Santa Maria, after Columbus' ship, across the Atlantic.

The Grumman "Duck" was a 1931 seaplane design. On water it floated on a large center float, while smaller floats under the wings helped to balance the aircraft. The "Duck" was an amphibian with retractable landing gear, a new feature at the time.

GRUMMAN J2F "DUCK"
Length: 34 ft (10.4 m)
Wingspan: 39 ft (11.9 m)
Speed: 190 mph (306 km/h)

CARRIER POWER

In World War II, the aircraft carrier became an important weapon at sea. Aircraft flying from carriers made all the difference in many battles. Even large battleships equipped with guns had difficulty surviving air attacks.

STRINGBAG ATTACK
The Fairey Swordfish, nicknamed "Stringbag," was a 1934 biplane. It was used by the British Navy during World War II to attack enemy battleships, cruisers, and submarines.

Aircraft Carrier

The importance of the aircraft carrier was realized during World War II. Before the war there were only about 30 of these big ships in the world. In 1945, when the war ended, the world total was more than 200, most of which were owned by the U.S. When U.S. forces attacked Okinawa, Japan, in April 1945, they were supported by more than 1,000 aircraft flying from 47 aircraft carriers.

On November 11, 1940, twenty British Swordfish bombers attacked the Italian navy in Taranto Harbor, in Italy, at around 10 p.m. Three Italian vessels were sunk and six were badly damaged. In May 1941, the German battleship Bismarck was heading into the Atlantic to attack **Allied convoys**. Swordfish torpedo bombers flying from the carrier HMS Ark Royal managed to damage the rudder of Bismarck. The damaged rudder made it impossible for the Bismarck to escape and it was sunk by Britain's Royal Navy the next morning. In the war over the Pacific, aircraft carriers played an important role. When U.S. forces attacked the Japanese held islands in the Pacific, aircraft carriers made it possible for them to have strong air support for the soldiers who had to wade ashore from the landing crafts. The U.S. Navy brought its own airfields, in the form of carriers, across the Pacific for the many air battles taking place over and around the islands.

GRUMMAN HELLCAT – WAR WINNER

The Grumman F6F Hellcat was the most important carrier fighter in World War II. It first flew in June 1942. About 12,272 Hellcats were built at the Long Island factory in New York before production ended in 1945. The Hellcat was a deadly fighter in the Pacific. Hellcat pilots destroyed more than 6,000 enemy aircraft. For each Hellcat lost, the U.S. Navy Hellcat pilots shot down nineteen enemy aircraft.

KAMIKAZE

Late in the war the Japanese took the desperate step of using kamikaze aircraft against U.S. ships. Kamikaze pilots tried to dive into the ships, exploding them with their planes.

SEA PATROL

During World War II, U-boats and aircraft were the greatest dangers to shipping. U-boats were slow underwater, so they needed to cruise on the surface to position themselves for their night attacks on Allied cargo ships.

A single aircraft patrolling in the sky could force several U-boats down, making it impossible for them to catch up with their convoy.
A Catalina flying boat could stay in the air 20 hours or more.

SUNDERLANDS
Short Sunderlands were the largest British-built flying boats of World War II. Sunderlands flew long patrols over the Atlantic, protecting convoys and attacking U-boats.

Carrier Subs
A few submarine carriers had their own aircraft in watertight **hangars**! A Japanese E14Y1 "Glen" float plane flying from a submarine was the only plane ever to bomb the United States. Twice in September 1942, Nobuo Fujita (shown above) dropped bombs on woods in Oregon. The Japanese hoped the forest fires would cause great panic. The panic did not happen, as most Americans never realized there had been an attack.

HEAVILY ARMED

On the Kawanishi H8K "Emily," the crew was protected by armor plating. This flying boat was also very heavily armed with five 20 mm machine cannons and four 7.7 mm machine-guns. Allied fighter pilots treated the "Emily" with extreme caution.

This made it an ideal aircraft for ocean patrols over slow moving ships. Catalinas were used to attack submarines too, but this was very dangerous, as the "Cats" were big, easy targets if the submarine stayed on the surface and tried to shoot down its attacker. The fastest flying boat during World War II was the Japanese H8K "Emily." It had a top speed of 290 miles per hour (467 km/h). It could stay airborne for over 25 hours and attack ships with bombs or torpedoes. Later versions of this flying boat had **radar** to help locate ships in dark and hazy conditions.

Blohm und Voss BV 138 MS

Degaussing ring

MINESWEEPER

The German Blohm und Voss BV 138 was converted to a flying **minesweeper**. A metal ring was fitted around the plane, and electric equipment generated a magnetic field around it. When flying low, this made mines explode without harming the aircraft. The BV 138 was often seen around the coasts of Europe. In Denmark the aircraft was nicknamed "Donald Duck."

TWILIGHT YEARS

During World War II, land planes became faster and more reliable. Airfields with paved runways were built everywhere. After the war, flying boats were less useful and became outdated.

SHORT SANDRINGHAM
The Sandringham had two passenger decks with sixteen seats on one and 24 on the other.

After World War II, the major airlines did not want flying boats anymore. Still, some wartime flying boats were used, such as the military Short Sunderland, which was converted into a passenger boat called the Short Sandringham. The Saro (Saunders-Roe) Princess, with a wingspan greater than today's Boeing 747, was a sad example of a flying boat that did not succeed. Construction on the Princess began during the war and the British government supported this giant, because it was planned as the ocean liner of the skies. Building it took far longer than expected and when the Princess took off on its first flight in 1952 it was already outdated. Plans for an even bigger 24 engine, five deck, 1,000 passenger flying boat were scrapped.

Airport
In 1944, the "Great West Aerodrome," later known as Heathrow Airport, in London, U.K., expanded for American B-29 bombers. When the war ended before the work was finished, it was decided that it should be used as London's main airport. In 1946, tents served as terminal buildings.

CUT UP FOR SCRAP

The huge Princess was finally junked in 1967. A businessman thought about using the hull as a moored coffee shop, but it ended up as scrap metal. It was a sad end to the dream of a flying ocean liner.

Large drag

Small drag

A HULL'S SHAPE

A flying boat hits the water's surface hard. The hull of the flying boat needs to be stronger and heavier than the fuselage of a regular airliner to withstand the pressure. The hull also needs to be able to sail on water, which means that it does not have the most streamlined shape for flying through the air. A flying boat will always be slower and heavier than a land plane carrying the same number of passengers.

SEA JETS

Flying boats were important sea weapons during World War II. After the war, some people thought that jet powered **military seaplanes would be needed in the future, both as fighters and as bombers.**

The idea of producing jet powered seaplane fighters resulted in experimental aircraft, such as the British Saunders-Roe SR/A1 and the U.S. Sea Dart. The Sea Dart was intended to fly faster than the speed of sound, but only managed to go **supersonic** in a dive. Jet fighter seaplanes were never a big success. In the **Cold War** years, both the **Soviet Union** and the U.S. built military craft to deter the other side from attacking. The U.S. Navy wanted nuclear bombers just like the U.S. Air Force, so the Martin P6M SeaMaster jet flying boat was developed and first flew in 1958. Its take-off weight was twice as high as a World War II four-engined flying boat, which made it hard to get off the water. Two **prototypes** crashed, but the program continued to build SeaMasters that could land to refuel and rearm from submarines. Eventually, the U.S. Navy cancelled this program.

SARO SR1

The single seat Saunders-Roe SR/A1 from 1947 was the world's first jet powered flying boat. The air intake was in the nose and sprays of water were separated from the air being let into the jet engines.

SEA DART

In 1948, the U.S. Navy wanted a supersonic seaplane fighter, because it feared that supersonic fighters would not be able to operate from aircraft carriers. The type ordered for test flying was the Convair XF2Y Sea Dart which first flew in 1953. Landing and take-off was on hydro-skis, which gave the pilot a very rough ride over the waves. The Sea Dart was never a success and the Navy soon realized that supersonic fighters could be flown from carriers.

Hydro-skis

AVOIDING SEA SPRAY

The SeaMaster nuclear bomber flew almost at the speed of sound. The air intakes for the jet engines were placed over the wings to protect them from salt water spray.

Polaris

The U.S. Navy armed its submarines with nuclear missiles, such as this Polaris. There was no way to stop these missiles once they were fired. They were a far greater threat than a jet flying boat, which could easily be shot down by enemy fighters. These missiles were a major reason why the SeaMaster, in spite of being an expensive and impressive aircraft, was already out of date when it went into service.

SEAPLANES TODAY

For some jobs, seaplanes are still the best kind of aircraft. Small flying boats and float planes are useful in remote areas with more lakes than runways. Flying boats are also used to fight forest fires.

There is nothing outdated about the Canadair CL-415 flying boat. The first flight of this Canadian fire fighting seaplane was in 1993 and the first customer received a CL-415 the next year. The CL-415 is used by fire fighting services all over the world.

Seaplane Kits
Ultralight aircraft (shown above on a dinghy) are flown on floats. Flying from water is fun, but you have to remember certain points. For example, if the engine is being warmed up prior to take-off, the seaplane will shoot forward, because it does not have brakes like a land plane.

FILLING THE TANKS
A Canadair CL-415 takes twelve seconds of skimming the surface to scoop 1,621 gallons (6,137 L) of water. Lifting off again it can still climb at 23 ft (7 m) per second.

GRUMMAN WIDGEON

The Grumman Widgeon is a small four seater amphibian which was first flown in 1940. They were in service during World War II and, amazingly, some of these old flying boats are still flying passengers today. Some fly people out to remote spots for North American wilderness adventures, while others are used for pleasure flights.

It can drop large amounts of water in places which are otherwise very difficult to reach. The CL-415 can refill its tanks from water as shallow as seven feet (two meters) and it can maneuver fast around river bends while doing so. The CL-415 pilot always tries to find a water source as close to the fire as possible. Even if the water source was seven miles (eleven kilometers) away from the fire, the CL-415 can still drop as much as 14,265 gallons (54,000 L) per hour on to the fire while flying at almost 249 miles per hour (400 km/h).

WATER BOMBS

The CL-415 drops a mixture of water and foam. The foam makes it easier for the pilot to see where the load lands. It also helps protect vegetation from the fire and is spread over a much wider area.

CARRIER PLANES

Shortly after World War II, jets began flying from aircraft carriers. Some were fighters, others bombers, while some flew special missions, performing tasks such as jamming enemy radar.

The FH-1 Phantom was the first U.S. jet fighter built for carrier operation. Design began during World War II and in 1946, it became the first U.S. jet to fly from a carrier deck. The Buccaneer was first flown in 1958, and went into service in 1962. It was a Cold War bomber that could carry a variety of weapons, including nuclear bombs. The Prowler is a strike aircraft. Its mission is to jam, or disturb, enemy radar and electronic signals. The Harrier is a strike aircraft that can land vertically. This makes it the only jet able to land gently on a carrier deck!

CARRIER CONTROL
There is never enough space on a carrier. The flight deck is a dangerous place for people who send off planes.

MCDONNELL FH-1 PHANTOM
Length: 38 ft 9 in (11.8 m)
Wingspan: 40 ft 9 in (12.4 m)
Speed: 479 mph (771 km/h)

BLACKBURN BUCCANEER
Length: 63 ft 5 in (19.3 m)
Wingspan: 44 ft (13.4 m)
Speed: 645 mph (1,038 km/h)

Grumman E2 Hawkeye

The Hawkeye first flew in the **Vietnam War** and is expected to remain in service until at least 2020. The Hawkeye is unarmed, but thanks to the big radar above the fuselage it can locate small enemy aircraft from 253 miles (407 km) away. The computers inside help the crew track up to 1,600 movements simultaneously. A surprise air attack on a U.S. carrier is not possible if a Hawkeye is flying above it! Landing on a deck is about the most difficult landing for a pilot. The deck is far shorter than a runway on dry land and in heavy seas it may move up and down by 26–33 ft (8–10 m).

SKI JUMP

The British Royal Navy Sea Harrier is a V/STOL aircraft, which means that it takes off from a short ski jump ramp and lands vertically. Sea Harriers do not need a huge flight deck. In 1982, the British used Sea Harriers, flying from small carriers, to provide air cover during the **Falklands War**.

Ski jump

GRUMMAN EA6-B PROWLER

Length: 59 ft 10 in (18.2 m)
Wingspan: 53 ft (16.1 m)
Speed: 651 mph (1,048 km/h)

BAE SEA HARRIER

Length: 47 ft 7 in (14.5 m)
Wingspan: 25 ft 3 in (7.7 m)
Speed: 736 mph (1,185 km/h)

ANGLED DECKS

World War II aircraft carriers had a straight flight deck. Aircraft risked crashing into other aircraft on the front part of the deck if they did not land properly. With fast jet landings, it became even more risky. The British invention of the angled flight deck allows pilots to go around again for another try at landing if they miss the first time.

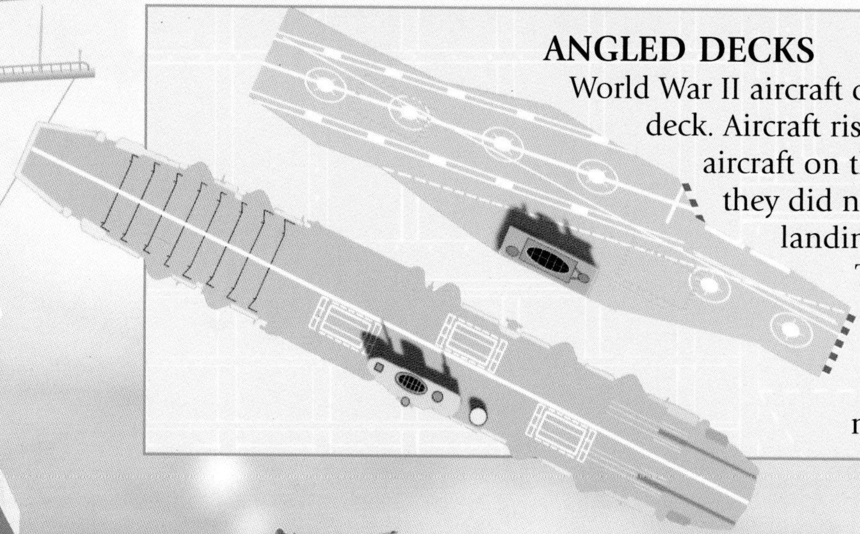

CATAPULT TAKE-OFF

A Tomcat is launched from a carrier deck. In two seconds the aircraft is accelerated from zero to around 150 mph (241 km/h)!

MODERN CARRIERS

Today's aircraft carriers are the biggest war machines ever built. The U.S. Navy uses the biggest ones. These huge U.S. aircraft carriers have 74–86 aircraft on board. The different types of aircraft fly many kinds of missions.

About half the aircraft on a super carrier are F/A-18 Hornets, which are used to attack enemy targets. F-14 Tomcats are fighters that protect U.S. forces from enemy aircraft. Using its long range radar, computer, and missiles, a Tomcat can track 24 targets and send six missiles simultaneously.

Tomcats shoot down enemy planes long before they get near the carrier. They work closely with the Hawkeye radar planes that spot the enemy on even longer distances. S3-B Viking tanker aircraft refuel the other aircraft in the air. Vikings also listen to enemy communications. Sikorsky HH-60H Rescue Hawk Helicopters are always in the air when planes land and take-off. Should something go wrong, they will pick up survivors quickly from aircraft that have crashed into the sea.

OCEAN POWER

Today, the most important job for the massive U.S. carriers is to support ground forces in land operations. The carriers are floating airfields, which makes it possible for the U.S. to employ air support around the world without needing airbases in different countries.

F-18

The F/A-18 Hornet is a multirole fighter. It can be armed with a wide variety of weapons, including smart bombs that hit targets very precisely, and the HARM (High Speed Antiradiation Missile), which homes in on enemy radar signals. The HARM forces the enemy to shut down their radar to avoid being destroyed.

FUTURE SEAPLANES

AIRFOIL FLAIRBOAT
German Airfoil Flairboats fly very low over the water, at around one foot (30 cm). Compared to other WIGs, the Flairboats are very simple to control. The Flairboats are classified as boats, but they do actually fly!

Future seaplanes could be very small and fly only at very low altitude. The plans for such craft, called WIG boats, have been under way since the 1960s.

Orlyonok
Soviet WIGs, such as the Orlyonok (above), were developed in secrecy as military transport and assault craft. They were known as Ekranoplans in the Soviet Union. The largest was powered by eight jet engines and had a wingspan of 131 feet (40 m) and a fuselage 348 feet (106 m) long. Seeing it on satellite spy photos, U.S. forces nicknamed it the Caspian Sea Monster because it flew training flights over the Caspian Sea in southeast Europe. It was the largest WIG ever.

WIG is short for Wing-in-Ground-Effect. Russian designer, Rostislav Alexeiev worked in ship building and imagined WIGs as ships flying just above the waves, where there would be no high drag from the water. German aircraft designer, Alexander Lippisch thought of the new seaplanes as flying boats that stayed down and flew on an air cushion under the wing. Both designed WIGs. WIGs fly equally well over land and water, but most are considered seaplanes. Over land, many obstacles such trees and houses would be in the way at such low altitude!

X-114
The X-114 from the 1960s was one of the last aircraft designed by Alexander Lippisch. He had designed gliders in the 1920s and 1930s. During World War II he designed the Me 163 rocket fighter.

Taking off and landing in rough weather is still a problem for WIGs. They also need a lot of power to accelerate and lift off from the water. Once up, they fly at the same speed as other aircraft, but use less fuel, which makes them cheaper to use. In 2003, the first commercial WIGs started flying passengers.

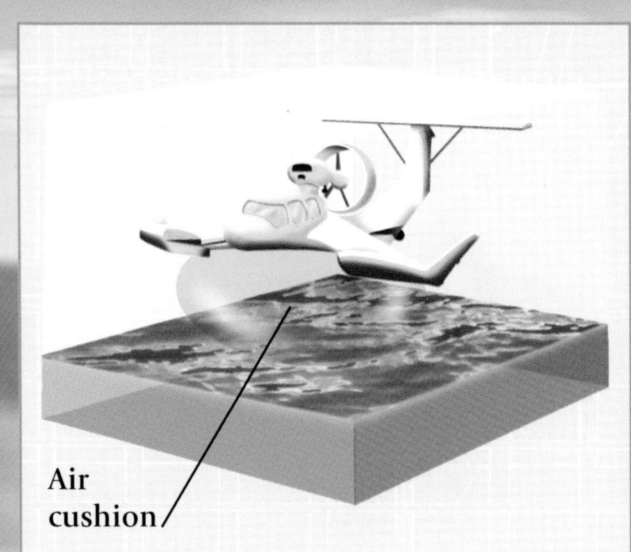

GROUND EFFECT
When a wing moves through the air, a low pressure area develops over the top, sucking the wing and aircraft up. At the same time, high pressure forms under the wing. When flying low, the high pressure acts as a cushion, helping lift the aircraft. This is called ground effect. By using ground effect, planes can fly with smaller wings that have less drag.

SPOTTERS' GUIDE

Seaplanes have been part of aviation history right from the start – from the wood and fabric Fabre Hydravion, to the all-metal jet powered SeaMaster. Seaplanes were seen as an important part of future air transportation in the 1930s. Then, after World War II, very few were designed. Today, modern flying boats and float planes are mainly designed and built as small planes for private use.

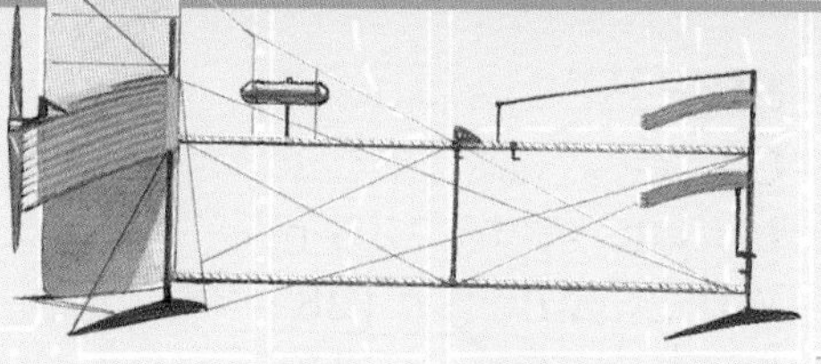

FABRE HYDRAVION
Country: France
Length: 27 ft 6 in (8.5 m)
Wingspan: 45 ft 6 in (14 m)
Speed: 50 mph (80 km/h)

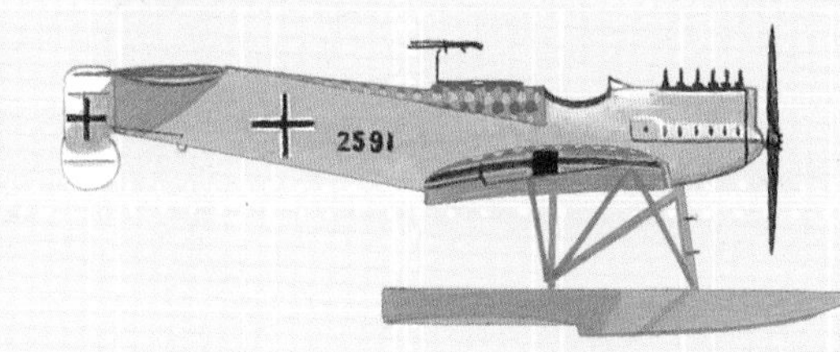

HANSA-BRANDENBURG W.29
Country: Germany
Length: 30 ft 6 in (9.4 m)
Wingspan: 43 ft 9 in (13.5 m)
Speed: 109 mph (175 km/h)

SARO PRINCESS
Country: Great Britain
Length: 148 ft (45.1 m)
Wingspan: 219 ft 6 in (66.9 m)
Speed: 358 mph (576 km/h)

FELIXSTOWE F.2A
Country: Great Britain
Length: 45 ft 10 in (14.1 m)
Wingspan: 94 ft 10 in (29.2 m)
Speed: 96 mph (154 km/h)

SHORT CALCUTTA
Country: Great Britain
Length: 66 ft (20.3 m)
Wingspan: 93 ft (28.6 m)
Speed: 118 mph (188 km/h)

FAIREY SWORDFISH MK II
Country: Great Britain
Length: 36 ft 4 in (11.1 m)
Wingspan: 45 ft 6 in (13.9 m)
Speed: 138 mph (222 km/h)

MARTIN P6M SEAMASTER
Country: USA
Length: 134 ft (40.8 m)
Wingspan: 102 ft 11 in (31.4 m)
Speed: 630 mph (1,010 km/h)

MC DONNELL DOUGLAS F-14 TOMCAT
Country: USA
Length: 62 ft (18.9 m)
Wingspan: (extended) 64 ft 1 in (19.5 m)
(retracted) 37 ft 7 in (11.4 m)
Speed: 1,584 mph (2,549 km/h)

INDEX

GLOSSARY

ALLIED Belonging to the nations that fought together during World War II, including Britain, France, the United States, and the Soviet Union.

ALTITUDE A height measured from sea level or the Earth's surface.

COLD WAR Political tension and military rivalry mainly between the U.S.A. and the Soviet Union from the end of World War II until the early 1990s.

CONVOYS Groups of ships traveling together for protection.

DRAG The force that pulls back on an aircraft.

FALKLANDS WAR A war between Great Britain and Argentina in 1982 over a group of islands in the Atlantic ocean off the coast of Argentina.

FLOAT A watertight structure that allows planes to sit on the water.

FUSELAGE The body of an aircraft in which the crew and passengers sit.

GALLEY The kitchen of a boat or an aircraft.

HANGAR A shed for housing or repairing aircraft.

HULL The frame or body of a ship.

JET POWERED Powered by a jet engine, which causes forward motion by forcing hot gases from a rear opening.

MINESWEEPER A warship designed for removing or setting off hidden mines.

PROTOTYPE The original model on which other types or models are based.

RADAR A device used for detecting enemy positions.

SOVIET UNION The Union of Soviet Socialist Republics, a group of countries under communist rule from 1922–1991.

SUPERSONIC Faster than the speed of sound.

TAXI To go at low speed along the ground or water.

TURBULENCE Stormy air caused by an air current moving against the flow of the main current.

U-BOAT A German submarine.

VIETNAM WAR A war in which the U.S. sent troops to help the south Vietnamese army fight the communist north from 1963–1975.

WORLD WAR I An international conflict involving many countries around the world which lasted from 1914–1918.

WORLD WAR II A war fought from 1939 to 1945 in which Great Britain, France, the Soviet Union, the United States, and other allies defeated Germany, Italy, and Japan.